BEGINNERS GUIDE – LEVEL

VIKING SWORD AND SHIELD FIGHTING

A Step-by-Step Book for learning to fight with Viking Sword and Centre-Gripped Round Shield. Incorporating safety concepts from an internationally known combat system practised world wide.

by Colin Richards

VIKING SWORD AND SHIELD FIGHTING
BEGINNERS GUIDE – LEVEL 1

Published in Germany
Arts of Mars Books
Colin Richards
31020 Salzhemmendorf
Tel. +49 (0) 5153/ 80 32 53
http:// www.ArtsOfMarsBooks.com

Author: Colin Richards
Design, Photos: Sandra Richards
Copy Editor: Charles Barnitz

ISBN 978-3-9811627-2-1

Printed in United Kingdom of Great Britain

Neither the author or the publisher assumes any liability for the use or misuse of information contained in this book. All martial arts, including historical can be dangerous and should only be practiced under the guidance of a qualified instructor, for personal development and historical study.

INTRODUCTION

Acknowledgments	4
About this Book	5
The Team	6
Before You Start	8

SECTION I – GENERAL

I. 1. Historical Background	10
I. 2 The Weapons	12
I. 3 The Safety Equipment	14
I. 4. Rules of Engagement	16
I. 5. The Sword and its Parts	18
I. 6. The Viking Shield and its Parts	19
I. 7. Strong and Weak	19
I. 8. How to Grip the Sword	20
I. 9. How to Grip the Shield	21
I. 10. Where to Look	22
I. 11. Breathing	22
I. 12. Information for Left Handed People	23

SECTION II – STEPPING

II. 1. Basic Stance	24
II. 2. Simple Forward Steps	25
II. 3. Simple Backward Steps	26
II. 4. Simple Diagonal Steps	27
II. 5. Simple Half Steps	28

SECTION III – USING SWORD AND SHIELD

III. 1. How to Strike Safely	30
III. 2. Our First Controlled Sword Attack	31
III. 3. The Natural Resting Position	32
III. 4. Attacking with Edge of the Sword	34
III. 5. First Strikes	34
III. 6. Basic Positions of Sword and Shield	40
III. 7. Parrying with the Sword	45
III. 8. Parrying with the Shield	50

SECTION IV – SINGLE PERSON DRILLS

IV. 1. Practising Strikes Against a Target Using a Half Step	56
IV. 2. Practising Strikes Against a Target Using a Full Step	62

SECTION V – PARTNER DRILLS

V. 1. Parrying with the Sword	68
V. 2. Parrying with the Shield	78
V. 3. Zonal Defense Using Sword and Shield	88
V. 4. Common Errors to Avoid	98
V. 5. Example of an Exchange of Blows	102

CONCLUSIONS 106

TABLE OF CONTENTS

ACKNOWLEDGEMENTS

We wish to extend our heartfelt thanks to all those countless and unnamed people who have helped us to become the martial artists that we are today.

We would also especially like to thank our wives for allowing us so much time to pursue our passion for martial arts even though they may have lost us for long periods, which of course may have been their plan all along!

I must thank my long time friend and confident Chris Halewood who not only appears in this book, but who also gave me the inspiration to begin writing this series.

The idea for beginners guide books that are sized so that you can take them anywhere was given to me by Bryan Tunstall of The Knight Shop International Ltd UK, so he deserves a special commendation. He really wants to see the community of Historical Martial Arts expand to its full potential and is full of ideas and support.

Special thanks go to my training partners and students who have helped me to refine my sword and shield teaching technique. These include Wolf-Bernd Eichler, Hanna Gäbelein, Jörg Weiss, Dominik Mennicke, Felix Reich, Melvin Raabe, Felix Seidel and Christopher Kunz.

Finally I must shower praises from on high on my wonderful wife Sandra Richards who has without doubt been the greatest help and impetus to keep me on the course to finish this book. Beyond that Sandra also accomplished the exacting feat of making the whole design and layout!

Colin Richards, Chris Halewood and Sandra Richards hope everyone will find this book useful, and we welcome comments and questions.

Colin Richards
Salzhemmendorf, Germany
April 2011

This is the first book in the Beginners series that uses an innovative design of the time-line. The first time we used this design feature was in the book *Fiore Dei Liberi 1409, Wrestling and Dagger* which was hailed as a breakthrough in the design of martial arts books. Following the techniques in a time-line helps the student visualise the sequence of movements better.

This book is intended as an beginners guide to learning to fight safely with the Early Medieval centre gripped round shield used primarily with a single handed Early Medieval sword or long sax (single edged sword), though any single handed sword can be used. The principles taught in this book can be employed with other weapons such as the single handed axe, the short sax and the single handed spear although the actual technical use of the weapon will be slightly different in each individual case.

The method shown in this book is based on a system which has been used in re-enactment or simulated combat in Europe since the late 1970's and has been further refined to incorporate new information and techniques arising out of the study of Historical European Martial Arts. These methods can be used in Stage Combat also.

Thus this system in its entirety can be used for study of actual techniques from the period in question or as a simulated combat system which incorporates safety, technical expertise and correct historical use of weapons. You can also use this system to learn how to make very visually appealing Stage Combat fights. The user determines the end result, by altering the criteria of use from Historical Study to Stage Combat to Re-enactment.

By adopting internationally accepted rules, safe combat can take place between two or more people in a relatively safe environment. A brief outline of these rules can be downloaded from our web site: **www.artsofmars.com**

This is the first in a series of three Beginner books on this subject, each of which will cover another aspect of the fight, and will increase in complexity so that any one can learn in simple stages the basic principles of this combat art. We start you off with simple attacks and defences, control of the weapon, stepping and judgement of distance. This is the core upon which everything else will be built.

Further we will release in the future Student Level Guides which will develop the basic principles and enhance the skills of the student to a higher level. All books will be supported with video material relative to the level of study undertaken.

We hope that you find this book useful and we would welcome reviews or comments. Please send all comments and reviews to: **info@artsofmars.com**

Please note that this book is written in British English.

Colin Richards

Born in Liverpool, England, Colin has been interested in weapons, warfare and military history for as long as he can remember. His first steps in martial arts took place 33 years ago when he studied Aikido and various other Asian martial arts.

Reenactment & Military History
(1981 – 1986)

In 1981 Colin took up re-enactment combat with steel blunt weapons, researching into early Anglo-Saxon combat techniques with the "The English Settlement Society" at Newcastle upon Tyne University. This were he met and made friends with Chris Halewood. See later.

During this research he learnt as much as possible from others in the field and through personal endeav-

our he became one of the training officers of the group. This group subsequently, has been instrumental in producing five books on the subject Military History of Early Anglo-Saxon England.
Research of Historical European Martial Arts
(2000 - 2011)

He has been researching into other Historical European Martial Arts for 11 years now. His main interest lies with the following treatises and areas of research:
Viking and Anglo-Saxon Sword and Shield combat AD 400 to AD 1100. Primary research into combat with round and kite shaped shields used in conjunction with other weapons, sword, axe, spear, sax.

The treatises of the fifteenth century Italian Master at Arms, Fiore dei Liberi, which includes wrestling, dagger, one handed sword, two handed

sword, sword in armour, pole axe in armour, spear, combat on horseback.

The fourteenth century treatise titled in the Royal Armouries Library as 1.33. This manuscript is from around AD 1300 (the oldest of the western European martial arts treatises yet found. Includes: Sword and Buckler combat (small shield).

Colin has taught over well over 2500 people in reenactment fighting and historical martial arts. Having created the Arts of Mars Historical Martial Arts Academy in 2005 he now has over 40 regular students in 4 permanent schools in the Hannover area of Germany.

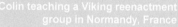

Colin teaching a Viking reenactment group in Normandy, France

Sandra Richards

Sandra is an architect and fully trained carpenter and therefore has been involved in design for many years. In the course of working as an architect she also developed skills in design of newsletters and larger more complex booklets.

In 2007 she came up with an innovative design for our first martial arts book, using landscape format and a time-line to display martial arts techniques in sequence to make it easier for readers to learn technique. This brilliant design was hailed as a great improvement over the standard portrait layout used in so many martial arts books.

Sandra adopts this landscape format in the Beginner's Guides Books, a tried and tested design for easier learning. She is responsible for the layout and design of the book and takes of all photographs, plus general encouragement and ideas.

Chris Halewood

Chris has been re-enactment fighting since 1980, first with English Civil War period groups and subsequently became more interested in Migration Era and Pre-Feudal warfare.

In 1981 he was a prominent member of the "The English Settlement Society" at Newcastle upon Tyne University. This were he met and made friends with Colin Richards.

He had trained previously in Kendo and fencing, but he decided to focus his energy on the spear, sword and shield fighting of the Anglo-Saxon and Viking periods.

He is still an active member of the re-enactment scene and gives courses on the use of spear and shield.

THE TEAM

7

The Aim of the Book

Firstly the aim of this book and all our books and DVD's is to develop interest in Historical European fighting techniques.

Secondarily the idea is either to be able to use those techniques in a comparatively safe and authentic fighting style, or to use them for further research into the interpretation of Historical European Martial Arts.

Thirdly these books can be used as preparation for training in Stage Combat.

The fighting system described in this and future Beginner's Guide books is based on very simple concepts. We break the complexity of combat into five simple attack zones defended by five simple defences. In future books we will expand these attack zones and defences, though not by much. What will change is the number of different attacking methods and the number of defensive alternatives; basically combining what you know already in different ways to produce new techniques.

No matter why you wish to study this weapon combination, of prime importance in every case is control of the weapon and shield. The method of control is described and shown in this book and we advise that every student learns this method perfectly so that the chance to make mis-takes which cause injury in actual simulated fighting is reduced to an absolute minimum. There are four contributors to safety described in this system. Remember these guidelines are as important for the use of the shield as for the sword.

The shield is a dangerous weapon if used to strike and can easily break bones, especially in the hands. Do not strike with the shield!

Firstly and most importantly is to have absolute control of the weapon we are attacking with. We "pull" the blows on contact, controlling their forward force almost completely. This can only be achieved by correct application of technique.

Secondly, we recommend that you use blunt plastic weapons to reduce the potential for harm.

Thirdly, we wear protective equipment on areas which may be damaged easily.

Fourthly, certain areas of the body are forbidden targets depending upon the level of protective equipment worn. If you fight without head and neck protection these targets are absolutely forbidden. *In this guide certain attack techniques are also forbidden, including thrusts to any part of the opponent.*

This system has been tried and tested for over 30 years by thousands of people using blunt steel weapons in free fight conditions, and the number of injuries requiring hospitalisation has been seen to be very low. In the hands of responsible and sensible people *no* injuries should occur at all. Always train and fight in conditions of good light and good footing and with plenty of unobstructed space.

Companion Video

Soon Arts of Mars will be releasing a companion DVD to go with this book, so you can really see it all in operation before you go out and practise using the book as a reminder.

Companions in Arms

The culture that surrounds any form of recreation involving fighting is wonderful. When you enter combat with someone you develop a special type of friendship and a powerful respect for them. You both know that you are capable of seriously hurting the other person, so that you have to modify the force of your blows and also your intention. You have to be in control of yourself at all times. Only after you have entered the world of historical armed combat will you realise this for yourself.

We wish you a extremely pleasant and safe experience using the system on offer in this series of books.

How to Use this Book

This book is organised in a simple manner. Each section starts with a few notes that apply to every position in that section, often to the whole book! These are found in these light green shaded areas.

These notes are followed by pictures which follow in Time Sequence, from left to right. Most pictures have relevant text above. Time sequence pictures lie on a green horizontal stripe.

Sometimes in the partner drill section we give a picture at the end of a sequence which shows the actual relative distance between the combatants at the end of the movement. These pictures are only for your reference, they are not part of the technique.

Read the text, follow the pictures, and then copy as best you can.
After three or four views you should have the basic position and movements in your head. Repeat as many time as you need to.

Also look out for our companion DVD's which cover exactly the same subject and level. These help you to visualise the movements better and then you can practise outside using the book as your guide!

Grid Lines in the Pictures

Most pictures show a sequence of grid lines on the floor as a visual reference so that you can better see the distance and angles of steps.

The first to second line is based on a half step. The second to third line is based on a full step. The third to fourth lines are based on the sword length to the opponent.

SECTION 1 – GENERAL

HISTORICAL BACKGROUND

There is not much written down from the old warriors about the use of the centre gripped round shield, so the methods shown here are derived from knowledge of the weapons and an application of martial arts principles coupled with experimentation and 30 years experience of what works and what does not.

We are lucky though that an old fencing master from Italy called Di Grassi 1594 wrote a combat treatise with techniques described for a centre gripped rectangular shield. He give far too much information to repeat here, except to say that he considered defending against cuts so easy that he was not even going to discuss it and only concentrate on defending against thrusts!

We only show cuts in this book so based on what a sword master said in AD 1594 it is going to be easy to defend yourself with a shield! With the correct application of technique, it is.

There are other techniques from other combat treatises which deal with similar weapons systems that have been incorporated in this system. References to these techniques will be included in the Student Guide series.

Di Grassi's book dealt with many weapons including swords and shields and bucklers. With large shields he emphasised thrusts over cuts.

His large centre gripped shield was rectangle in shape and held with the point of the rectangle uppermost. His sword was somewhat longer than an normal Viking sword.

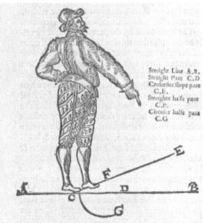

Streight Line A,B,
Streight Pace C,D
Crokeder llope pace
C,E.
Streighter halfe pace
C,F.
Circuler halfe pace
C,G

betweene the Target & bodie of the enimie, with the encrease of a pace of the right foote: the which thrust will safely speede the enimie, if his bodie be not first voided. The selfe same thrust may be deliuered in this high ward, standing with the right foote behind,

The defence of the high warde, at Sworde & square Target.

HE forefaid thrust may easily be warded, if in the verie time that it commeth it be encountred with the high poynt of the Target, but yet with that side which bendeth towardes the right hand. And as foone as the enimies sworde is come one handfull within the Target, it must be strongly beaten off by the Target towardes the right hand, increasing the same instant a left pace. Then with as great an increase of a pace of the right foote as may be possible, a thrust vnderneath most be giuen, already prepared, because a man ought to stand at the lowe warde for the warding of the thrust abouehand.

The hurt of the broad warde, at Sworde and square Target.

IN this warde likewise, the enimie may be inuested on the poynt of the sworde, by going forwardes as straightly as is possible, and by striking quickly before the enimie. For the Target (whose charge is only to defend) is fo great, that it may eafily warde all edgeblowes, & thofe chiefely which come from the knee vpwardes. Father, when a blowe is pretended to be deliuered, it is manifeft, that a thruft doth enter by a more narrowe ftraight than any edgeblowe doth.

L 2　　　　And

THE WEAPONS

We recommend the following weapon range manufactured by The Knights shop in the UK. Arts of Mars was consulted on the design along with many other organisations, though the main influence on the creation and design of this excellent range of martial arts equipment was Dave Rawlings of the Boars Tooth Academy London and rightly bear his name as a sign of quality.

Weapon Contact with the Opponent

No hit or contact should cause injury or lasting pain, if this occurs communicate immediately with your opponent and tell them the situation. If you have control of your weapons there should be no damage caused. *See Controlling the Weapon.*

Note: Sometimes through a combination of events even the most controlled blow can cause bruising or worse, this is why we advise that you always wear protective equipment for all target zones and the hands and arms up to and including the elbow. We also recommend protection for the groin, in the form of some sort of hard material.

The Dave Rawlings Red Dragon Range

While learning to fight with weapons we recommend starting with plastic swords. These have the advantage of having a thick safe edge and flexible point, a good weight and they are very durable.

Please note that those shown in the pictures may not exactly match those now supplied as different models have been introduced and others have been discontinued. The swords pictured in this book were hand made for us by the Knights Shop.

These plastic swords can be obtained from:
www.ArtsOfMarsBooks.com or
www.TheKnightshop.co.uk

Metal Weapons

Usually experienced warriors fight with blunt steel weapons that are manufactured out of spring steel to a high quality. We do not recommend these type of weapons to new practitioners.

The Shield

This can be made from a variety of materials though for training and fighting we use shields made from plywood edged with raw hide. These vary in diameter from 60 cm 24 inch to 1 metre 39 inch. On no account should you ever use a shield to strike an opponent.

SECTION I. 2.

THE SAFETY EQUIPMENT

We recommend that you use as minimum protection a helm, padded gloves and lower arm guards. Later in your study you may like to increase protection for your body by using padded garments or hockey or lacrosse armour. This allows the combatants to strike with slightly less control of the blows.

Further-more, we advise the use of a fencing/ lacrosse hard throat and groin protection for all combat simulation. These can also be obtained from artsofmars.com.

Check your safety equipment from time to time for wear and tear. Some foam stuffing can deteriorate after many impacts, becoming almost useless.

Helmet

This is a safety helmet used for fencing to protect the head and eyes. These are the strongest normally made which can take 1600 Newtons of force. These are not normally worn in re-enactment fighting. You can substitute an historically accurate metal helm with or without face protection.

Gloves

Strong padded gloves should be used to protect the hands and fingers from accidental impacts. At the moment we use Lacrosse and Hockey gloves or self-made triple layer gloves. In the future we should have available purpose-made gloves for sparring and fighting. See our web site for details.

The Pell

Warriors of antiquity used to hone their skills and control by striking a pole stuck firmly in the ground, which is called a pell. The pell is a great training tool, and has many uses.

We have constructed a simple one to use in this book. By placing different tape markings on it to represent different targets, such as head, shoulder and thigh, you can learn accuracy and control skills on it.

You can also hone your distance judgement by placing the pell at different distances and striking from there. Today you can use a tree or an hanging tire, or a stout pole stuck firmly in the ground. The pell is absolutely essential for learning accuracy, control and distance judgement. We cannot recommend them highly enough.

Arm Guards

Simple arm protection is made from thick leather with a projection for the elbow joint. You can use Lacrosse and Hockey armour, which will also be available from our web site.

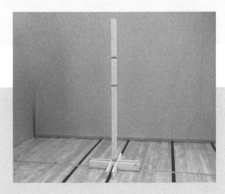

THE RULES OF ENGAGEMENT

In the Beginners Guide books, regardless of your level of protection, we suggest that you keep to the following rules as regards Hit Zones if you wish to use the system for simulated combat. Later modifications will be added.

Simple Rules Of Engagement

Any strike that hits a zone kills the opponent and the fight ends! First person contacting with the strike kills first! Striking at almost the same time causes a double kill result and the fight ends for both combatants.

The hit zones for the beginners guides are limited to the torso, the shoulders down to the elbow, and the legs down to the knees, not including the groin area.

Other hit location such as the hands and lower legs can be added as you wish, to increase the relative realism of the Rules. You should note however, these areas need adequate protection from injury in the form of armour unless you are fighting with very experienced opponent's.

These rules have been designed with safety in mind. They are easy to change though please take care to make safety your prime concern.

Zone 1 – The Head

There should be absolutely no contact with an unprotected head or neck – the weapon is stopped 20cm/ 8 inches from contact. Why should we practise this attack and defence?

Zone 1 is always taught and practised so that if you should fight with someone who for whatever reason targets your head, you have already programmed yourself to respond with a defence even though you hope never to use it at this stage.

This was considered a fight ending blow, even if you did not penetrate the helm, it could knock him senseless! Though the unprotected head and neck are not actively targeted, the whole of the torso of the body can be.

Zone 2 – The Left Shoulder

This zone should be contacted by diagonal blows at approximately 30 degrees to the vertical, striking between the edge of the left shoulder and the start of the neck from above, though not including the neck. This zone includes the upper arm above the elbow.

This is the real cleaver cut, it is said that warriors could cut the man through to the hip on occasion!

Zone 3 – The Right Shoulder

This zone should be contacted by diagonal blows at approximately 30 degrees to the vertical, striking between the edge of the right shoulder and the start of the neck from above, though not including the neck. This zone includes the upper arm above the elbow.

A back hand strike to the shoulder or neck could end the fight easily, incapacitating the sword arm, or taking off the head!

Zone 4 – The Left Thigh

This zone should be contacted by diagonal blows at approximately 60 degrees to the horizontal, striking the thigh between the knee and the hip from below, though not including any part of the knee.

The sword used under arm could cut through the thigh muscle or into the stomach, collapsing the opponent in an instant!

Zone 5 – The Right Thigh

This zone should be contacted by diagonal blows at approximately 60 degrees to the horizontal, striking the thigh between the knee and the hip from below, though not including any part of the knee.

This swing from below cannot only cut the thigh muscle through or if the hand is in the way it can cleave the swordsman's hand from his arm!

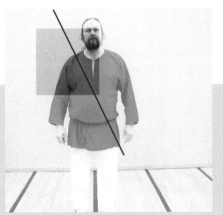  

The angle of 30 degrees is used as this prevents damage to the collar bone and prevents the sword bouncing into the head if the blow was at a flatter angle.

THE SWORD
AND ITS PARTS

The sword has two main parts, divided into the **handle** and the **blade.**

The handle has three parts, the grip, the pommel, which is used as a counter weight to the blade, and the cross guard, which is there to protect the hand and fingers.

The blade has a point and two edges [unless single bladed] and two flat surfaces known as the "flats".

The part of the blade from the tip to the middle is called the Weak of the blade. That part from the middle to the handle is known as the Strong of the blade.

We always attempt to parry a blow with the Strong of the blade and strike with the Weak of the blade, more toward the tip than the middle.

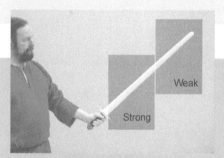

This picture gives a good idea of the Weak and Strong of the blade.

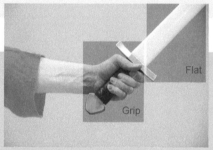

The grip is divided into the pommel, the cross guard, and the handle. The sword blade has two sides called the flats.

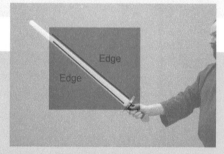

The two edges lie upon the upper and lower part of the flats, and are usually sharp. The point can be round or more pointed, as in Viking times.

THE VIKING SHIELD AND ITS PARTS

STRONG AND WEAK

The centre gripped early medieval round shield is usually made with a central boss of iron attached to three or more planks of wood.

The planks are covered in linen or other cloth and the rim protected with raw hide leather. We deal here with flat boarded shields though there were concave round shields used as well.

We make things a little easier by making our shields from three-ply wood, which is easier to find and cheaper.

When gripped in the centre, the hand is usually thumb up. Due to the natural strength of the wrist, the shield is usually Strong in the upper and lower quarters of the shield and Weak in the right and left quarters of the shield. The shield is also stronger nearer to the boss and weaker nearer the rim.

Remember do not use the shield as a weapon to strike.

This refers to the amount of leverage that can be applied to a weapon. Leverage is more easily applied to a weapon furthest away from the controlling hand. So that part furthest away from the hand is the weakest part and that nearest the hand is the strongest part. This applies to all weapons and no less to shields.

The shield has strong and weak areas depending upon the alignment of the wrist and grip to the board. It is also stronger near the boss and weaker near the rim.

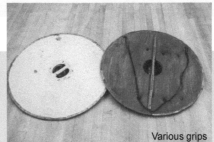

Various grips

There are various different ways of making the grip, either from wood or metal.

HOW TO GRIP THE SWORD

The sword is gripped in the hand so that the top of the handle of the sword lies along the muscle group just under the thumb, and at the base of the palm, so that the sword sits in what we term the Natural Resting Position [NRP].

To make the NRP just put your normal sword hand out and place the sword grip in it in the position described above. Grip the sword sufficient to hold it in place against a slight pull of the blade. Be relaxed. On no account hold it very tight and end up with white knuckles!

The angle that the sword sits at naturally is YOUR Natural Resting Position! This may be slightly different for each individual. We always end in this position when striking, whatever the angle of cut. The wrist joint is straight with no bends.

Stop the wrist in this position with every cut or parry. This gives you good control of the weapon, this will be easier after a few repetitions. Keep relaxed and let the sword do the work, then you can fight all day without a rest! If you find this difficult, find a lighter sword. The sword should be around one kilogram.

The line below shows where the grip should lie in a right handed person. Each persons position will be slightly different. Make sure it feels comfortable.

The position is exactly similar for the left handed person. This position should feel natural and comfortable.

A right handed person gripping the sword. With the wrist straight the sword sits at a natural angle.

HOW TO GRIP THE SHIELD

The handle is gripped in a natural way. We use the same approach as that with the sword so that the grip lies along the muscle group under the thumb, and at the base of the palm.

The shield will also sit in its own Natural Resting Position [NRP].
With a large shield you may find you have to angle the wrist a little to bring the face of the shield to the vertical.

Keep relaxed and holding the shield will not become a burden and when struck the shield will find its own stable position against the oncoming blow!

The natural strength of the wrist will absorb some of the force of the blow, as will the mass of the shield.

We demonstrate two positions of the thumb. One on the grip and the other on the shield board. This is purely personal preference. Both are equally good.

Always rest with the shield closer to the body and move the shield out to more or less arms length for all parries.

Remember also at the moment of the parry the blow is still at full force!

WHERE TO LOOK

BREATHING

While you are learning the strikes and parries you may find it important to look at the weapon or shield to see if your technique is correct. After a while you should use peripheral vision while attacking, while defending look directly at the opponent's attacking weapon hand. Peripheral vision is when you see things with the outer part of the iris, without looking directly at the object.

As much as possible, breath in a normal and relaxed rhythm, though in combat be sure to exhale while striking and inhale while making the next action. Inhale through the nose and exhale through the mouth.

Colin teaching a Viking reenactment group in Normandy, France

Colin teaching the Historical Martial Arts Group "Ochs e.V." Munich, Germany

INFORMATION FOR LEFT HANDED PEOPLE

This entire system works in exactly the same way for people who use the sword in the left hand. Just reverse the orientation in the descriptions. Left becomes right and vise versa.

Generally in a fight between opposite handed opponent's, because both are seeking the un-shielded side, the right handed person moves to his right and the left handed person moves to his left. This is important to remember. Left handed people have a slight advantage in that they often fight right handed opponent's and therefore gain a lot of experience and useful tricks.

The opposite is true of right handed people, they seldom get to fight against a left handed opponent's. If you have time, we recommend that you learn to fight with both hands, sword or shield.

Left handed people should follow the same principles as laid down in the guide and therefore should have no problem performing the techniques as shown, though of course mirrored.

End of the Viking Sword and Shield seminar at "Ochs e.V." Munich, Germany

SECTION II – STEPPING

BASIC STANCE

Place both feet together so that the feet are under the shoulders and and take one normal step forward.

For good balance, your knees should be roughly under your shoulders and slightly bent.

We recommend that new practitioners maintain their weight evenly distributed over both legs, while in this basic stance. Don't be too square on to the opponent.

Remember, you may want a broader stance to suit your style of fighting! Experiment with the width and breadth of your stance and the position of your feet to suit yourself.

There are several simple steps covered in this book. Though there are many other stepping possibilities, here we only cover those that are absolutely essential. Everybody makes these types of steps in daily life, we just do not realise we are doing them! There are no magic steps in martial arts, we just have to be more precise and more aware of how we ordinarily move.

Movement in combat is vitally important and will greatly determine how well you fight! Practise footwork in all sorts of terrain and become sure-footed in whatever conditions you find yourself. Move with every cut and every parry, and you will quickly become a great warrior, no one will hit you!

One consequence of this stance is that the upper body and hips are turned away. This leaves one side of the body further away, and one side closer to the opponent.

The slightly turned body also means that you present a smaller target to the opponent. Experiment with different angles of body position in your fighting.

SIMPLE FORWARD STEPS

The first stage in any step is shifting the weight to the stationary foot and then moving the other foot to the required position. Remember to step so that the knees are about shoulder width apart, especially if fighting on grass.

Turn your body slightly so that you are not square on to the direction of movement. The second step repeats this movement with the other leg. Keep it simple – keep it shorter rather than longer if on grass!

Do not slide the feet along the floor, this may work in the training room, but it only invites injury in combat in real terrain.

Start in the normal stance position.

After the first full step, your torso should be pointing approximately 45 degrees from straight ahead. Balance in the middle.

After the second full step your torso should be pointing approximately 45 degrees from straight ahead on the other side. This makes you a smaller target and increases reach on one side.

SIMPLE BACKWARD STEPS

This is the opposite of forward stepping, the weight is placed over the rear foot, the front foot moves backward, again stepping so that the knees are about shoulder width apart. Turn your body slightly so that you are not square on to the front. Subsequent steps repeats this movement, alternating legs.

Check behind you when going backward, by glancing over the shoulder of the leg which is behind, using your peripheral vision. Use repeated backward step with care, **think before going back!**

Remember to start in a basic stance and make sure you go straight back along a line. Later you can vary the angle of backward movement.

After the first full step backwards your torso should be pointing approximately 45 degrees from straight ahead.

After the second full step your torso should be pointing approximately 45 degrees from straight ahead on the other side. This makes you a smaller target and increases reach on one side.

SIMPLE DIAGONAL STEPS

Diagonal steps are often seen in combat. As shown in the pictures below, a diagonal step requires two actual steps to complete the movement.

Note that diagonal steps are not fixed in angle or length of step. Also, a diagonal step does not advance you as far as a regular forward step, so to score a hit on a diagonal step, you must begin closer to your opponent, or take a bigger step.
They are also more complex to perform than normal forward steps, so remember your balance!

The first step is off to the side and forward at an approximate angle of 45 degrees though the angle is not fixed, we can vary it as we wish according to the situation.

The second step is made to maintain the balance and the orientation to the opponent.

Notice the width of step is the same as the forward and backward steps, with the knees under the shoulders.

This step give real versatility to your fighting style! You can vary the angle and the length to determine where you will be in relation to your opponent stroke for stroke!

Here is an example of a diagonal step to the left from another viewing angle. Start in the basic stance.

Take a normal step at an angle of about 45 degrees, going to the side as well as forward.

Finish the step by moving the back leg behind the front leg into normal stance while orientating yourself with the opponent.

SIMPLE HALF STEPS

This is very good to close distance with the same leg forward. You can adjust distance with this step and control orientation. Depending upon your style, you might want to use this step quite often!

Some people call these steps adjustment steps or fencing steps because they are often used in sports fencing. The main thing to remember is that people make these steps automatically in many normal situations. Therefore in combat, after a little experience, you will find yourself doing these steps without thinking.

Tactically, think about them as a way to keep orientation to the enemy, say for instance you have two opponent's and you want to keep the shield side forward for maximum shield protection.

Start in the normal stance. You can do these steps with either leg forward. Reverse the process to go backward.

Extend the front foot forward about half the width of a normal step. Keep in balance. Do not drop the weight on the forward foot.

Bring the rear leg up to re-establish the normal balanced stance.

SECTION III
USING THE SWORD AND SHIELD

HOW TO STRIKE SAFELY

Striking safely is all important, we use a simple system that everyone can learn quickly.

We always strike to the same Natural Resting Position (NRP) as shown in Gripping the Sword.

This position maintains a straight wrist, which means you always come to an exact position whatever your attack, a position you know!

This means your sword should always come to the same position as well. Controlling your hand controls the sword!

Once you have learnt the Natural Resting Position, all you have to judge is the distance to the target. Stop the sword in the NRP just before the target.

After a little practise you will be able to stop it on the target, with almost no impact!

This sequence shows a simple attack without a step against the left shoulder of the imaginary opponent. We start in a guard position.

Half way through the strike the body has twisted to the left using the legs and hips and finally the shoulders.

The strike lands with the edge about 20cm/ 8 inches from the point. Note the wrist position is straight. Try this out a few time to get the feel of the sword in your hand.

OUR FIRST CONTROLLED SWORD ATTACK

If we swing the sword from over the right shoulder forward so that the hand ends level with the breast bone, we have made a cut from above to below. Stop the sword and hand with the wrist straight as above. This is the NRP.

Important: we swing from the shoulder and utilise the elbow not the wrist! The wrist is held straight, though it remains relaxed.

You now have learnt the exact angle that **your** sword will always end at with every similar swing.

You will learn all the other cuts in a similar manner.

The next stage in this system is to be able to judge the distance to the target. You can learn that in Single Person Drills 1 and 2.

Here is an example with pictures. Guard Position 2 making a Left Shoulder Attack to Zone 3. Start with the sword high over the right shoulder with the sword pointing slightly out to the side.

Swing the sword forward in a slight arc, twisting the hips and shoulders toward the centre line.

31

THE NATURAL RESTING POSITION

Finish with the sword hand level with the breast bone and the last 20 cm/ 8 inch of the sword blade level with the temple of your head. Your wrist joint is straight, you are in the NRP! Here are close ups of all the NRP's we are using in this guide.
Note the position of the wrist joint! This gives a precise position that your sword will end in for every strike. Through practise we can learn to place the sword in contact with the target without much impact!

Take time to practise these movements, it will serve you well.

Remember as you practice the cuts to check that your wrist is in the correct position every time until it becomes second nature.

We use the NRP because of safety consideration and so that your wrist has the correct structure bio-mechanically. This is a strong position for the wrist and the structure makes it less likely that you can sprain or otherwise injure the wrist.

A good fighter has a good structure both bio-mechanically and mentally.

Attack Zone 1 - Head
Here we have attacked the opponent's head, with a vertical strike. You can see the wrist is straight and the sword is in he NRP.

Attack Zone 2 - Left Shoulder
This attack was against the opponent's left shoulder. This strike was a diagonal cut from right to left. The wrist is in the same position though slightly turned toward the right.

Attack Zone 3 - Right Shoulder

An attack from left to right at the right shoulder of the opponent ends in the NRP. A natural consequence of this is that the hand is turned slightly toward the left.

Attack Zone 4 - Left Thigh

We see here an cut toward the left thigh of the opponent from below. The wrist is still straight though turned about 150 degrees to the right.

Attack Zone 5 - Right Thigh

This cut is made from below to the right thigh of the opponent and ends with the wrist straight and again in the NRP. The back of the hand is turned to the left.

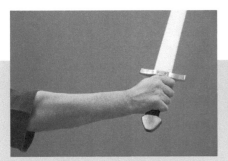

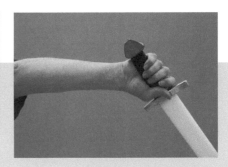

SECTION III. 3.

ATTACKING WITH THE EDGE OF THE SWORD

FIRST STRIKES WITH THE SWORD

Attacking the Head

Remember contacting a head which is not protected by at least strong helmet and neck guard will lead to some form of injury, do not do it!

Even when wearing protection control the blow so that minimal contact is made. Your friend's head is at stake!

Practise the strike in mid air and imagine an opponent about the same size as you in front of you.

This will give you a good feel for swinging the sword and also build confidence in your sword control.

Also practise cutting through the target and see where the sword finishes in its path. You should find that it often ends up in one of the guard positions that we cover later. This is very helpful and tactically important.

Remember in each of these strikes, start with the weight evenly distributed over both legs.
Always strike from the shoulder with the whole arm!

Stay relaxed and don't raise those shoulders: that is an obvious sign you are going to attack!

Do not drop the sword point behind you, it takes more time, and telegraphs to the opponent that you are making a strike.

Attacking with the point of the Sword - Thrusting

This will be covered in Beginners Guide Three.

Do not do it until you learn the technique!

34

A Strike to the Opponent's Head

Never contact an unprotected head or neck.

Guard Position 1

Sword above the side of the head, pointing upward, **do not** drop the sword point backward at the start of the move. Use a balanced stance, bend the knees.

Swing the sword forward, while shifting the weight over your front leg and twisting the hips and shoulders toward the centre line. Remember balance!

Step forward during the swing. This step should follow the swing of the sword smoothly.

Stop the sword swing as the foot lands. The sword swing stops within 20 cm/8 inches of the imaginary opponent's head [if unprotected] so that you would strike somewhere in the weak part of the sword. You should be in the NRP. Aim to strike the centre, adjust your aim if you were off line.

With this blow the warrior could have split the head in two! Please do not, as it will upset your friend. Watch that control.

A Strike to the Opponent's
Left Shoulder

Guard Position 2

Sword above the right shoulder, pointing upward. Keep arm, hand and blade in the same line, swing freely.

Swing the sword forward using movement at the shoulder, while shifting the weight over your front leg.

Step forward, the sword should be controlled at the end of the swing as the foot lands, strike with the weak of the sword. You should be in the NRP, the sword angled at about 30 degrees to the right of the vertical.

For a right handed swordsman, this strong left to right cleaving blow is the most natural to make and control.

A Strike to the Opponent's Right Shoulder

Guard Position 3

Sword above the left shoulder, point upward.

From the left shoulder swing the sword, while shifting the weight over your front leg and twisting the hips and shoulders toward the centre line.

While you are swinging the sword, step forward. The step and swing should be one smooth motion.

As the step ends the sword contacts the imaginary target, here the right shoulder. Stop in the NRP and the sword angled at about 30 degrees to the left of the vertical.

This is the third most powerful strike, and into the un-shielded side of a right handed person.

37

A Strike to the Opponent's Left Thigh

Guard Position 4

Sword below the right shoulder, pointing at the ground to the side, or behind; your preference. This cut tries to get in under the opponent's shield.

Swing the sword upward and forward, move your weight slightly forward, follow the cut with your hips and shoulders, turning toward the centre line.

As you swing/step, control the sword on contact with the opponent. The target is to strike the imaginary opponent in the left thigh with the weak of the sword. Finish in the NRP, the sword angled with the point a little toward the ground.

Hopefully you would have struck under the shield into the thigh or even under the arm pit! You can vary the target as you see fit.

A Strike to the Opponent's Right Thigh

Guard Position 5

Sword below the left shoulder, with the point toward the ground and behind. This swing tries to cut behind the opponent's shield.

Swing the sword forward with a slight upward arc, remember these swords were not twirled by the wrist. Turn the hips and shoulders inwards as you shift your weight forward.

Use the same system as the previous four cuts. Step with the cut, control the cut as the foot lands. Imagine the target, the right thigh, hit with the end third of the sword. Use the NRP to end with the sword point angled a little toward the ground.

Now you have made your first five strikes with the sword. The Warrior within is just waiting to get out!

BASIC POSITIONS OF THE SWORD AND SHIELD

Remember to always start with the weight distributed evenly over both legs, later guides will show your other weight positions that can be used.

The blade angle can be adjusted to suit your own style of fighting, though do not angle the sword too far behind you as this will increase the time needed to cut!

The shield is normally covering the

Over the Side of the Head

Guard Position 1
This is the starting position for making strikes to the opponent's head. The sword is over the top of the head with the blade angled a little behind the vertical.

The shield position is typically covering the left side and left shoulder, though try experimenting with slight variations, such as lowering it a little. Subtle changes in shield position can be used for advantage!

left shoulder, with the face of the shield angled at about 45 degrees to straight ahead. The front edge of the shield is level with the centre of the body. Adjust how much shield cover you want for your own style of fighting. Leaving part of the body uncovered entices the opponent to strike to your unprotected side and is known as an invitation!

Over the Right Shoulder

Guard Position 2

Start in this position for making strikes to the opponent's left shoulder. The sword hand is by the right shoulder as in the picture.

Lowering the shield entices the opponent to strike for you left shoulder! Raising it exposes the left thigh! Invitations can control your opponent's thinking.

Over the Left Shoulder

Guard Position 3

This position is used for making strikes to the opponent's right shoulder. The sword is held over the left shoulder with the blade inside the shield rim.

The shield can be held with the rim level with the shoulder, though you can hold it a little lower if this helps the sword arm to have a clear path to the target.

You are inviting the opponent to strike your right side. As you develop more skill you will be able to subtly vary what your shield is covering and make your invitations less easily read by your opponent.

Under the Right Shoulder

Guard Position 4

This position is used for making strikes to the opponent's left thigh. Hold the sword under the right shoulder with the point downwards and to the side. You can angle the blade further toward the rear.

The shield should be covering the left shoulder and side. You can use the same invitations as before.

Your aim is to strike under the opponent's shield.

Under the Left Shoulder

Guard Position 5

This position is used for making strikes to the opponent's right thigh. Hold the sword under the left shoulder, as best you can, with the point downwards and to the rear. The sword blade should be inside the shield rim.

The shield should be covering the left shoulder, though it can be slightly higher to facilitate the placement of the sword behind the shield.

Be careful with this position as your sword can become trapped behind your shield in certain circumstances.

PARRYING WITH THE SWORD

With all parries with the sword aim to catch the opponent's sword in the strong, the bottom half of the blade. Make sure also you are out of distance, should your parry fail. Do not worry about which leg is forward; the procedure is very similar.

Here we start in a neutral position, called Middle Guard in later guides.

Parrying Attacks to the Head

Sword Parry Position 1

Start with the sword in a guard or any other neutral position in your normal stance.

Bring the sword above your head and angle the blade so that it covers the whole width of your body from shoulder to shoulder. The point can slightly droop toward the floor.

Aim to catch the opponent's sword in the Strong of the blade. This is an excellent position to counter-attack from.

**Parrying Attacks to
the Left Shoulder**

Sword Parry Position 2
Start with the sword in any guard in your normal stance.

This is a waiting position called Low Middle Guard

Push the sword to the left side of your body with the sword hand slightly outside the width of your left shoulder, so that you are covered behind your sword. Extend the arm diagonally forward until there is still a slight bend at the elbow.

Make sure that the point of the sword remains on your centre line. Very Important!

Parry with the bottom half of the sword, pushing slightly against the opponent's weapon on contact. Do not bend the wrist joint if you can help it. Relax and use the natural spring in the wrist to absorb the shock of the parry.

Parrying Attacks to the Right Shoulder

Sword Parry Position 3

Take up any neutral position in your normal stance. The position below is a sword forward position that will be covered in the next guide called Middle Guard. Try different start positions for your sword.

The parry is made by pushing out the sword to the right side of your body with the sword hand slightly outside the width of your shoulder, so that you are covered behind your sword. Extend the arm diagonally forward so that there is still a slight bend at the elbow.

Make sure that the point of the sword remains on your centre line. Very Important!

Parry with the bottom half of the sword, pushing slightly against the opponent's weapon on contact. Do not bend the wrist joint if you can help it. Relax and use the natural spring in the wrist to absorb the shock of the parry.

Parrying Attacks to the Left Thigh

Sword Parry Position 4

Start with the sword in a guard or any other neutral position in your normal stance.

This is a waiting guard called Middle Guard.

Bring the sword to the left side of your body with the sword hand slightly outside the width of your shoulder, and the point of the sword pointing toward the floor, so that you are covered behind your sword. Extend the arm so that there is a slight bend at the elbow. You should see the Back of your sword hand!

Make sure that the point of the sword remains just outside the width of your body! Very Important.

Parry with the strong of the sword if at all possible, pushing slightly downwards against the opponent's weapon on contact. Do not bend the wrist joint if you can help it. Relax and use the natural spring in the wrist to absorb the shock of the parry.

Parrying Attacks to the Right Thigh

Sword Parry Position 5

Start with the sword in a guard position in your normal stance. The position below is a sword forward position that will be covered in the next guide called Middle Guard

Bring the sword to the right side of your body with the sword hand slightly outside the width of your shoulder, and the point of the sword pointing toward the floor, so that you are covered behind your sword.

Extend the arm so that there is only a slight bend at the elbow. You

should also be able to see the back of your sword hand! Do not see the palm as that gives your opponent an easy disarm!

Make sure that the point of the sword remains just outside the width of your body! Very Important.

Parry with the strong of the sword if at all possible, pushing slightly downwards against the opponent's weapon on contact. Do not bend the wrist joint if you can help it. Relax and use the natural spring in the wrist to absorb the shock of the parry.

PARRYING WITH THE SHIELD

Do not worry which leg is forward the procedure is very similar. Always move the shield as little as required and extend the arm as you parry. Make sure you can always see the opponent; do not blind yourself with the shield. All shield parries start with the shield covering the left shoulder and side, though you can vary the position according to your own fighting style and for invitations.

The basic stance is used in each start position.

Parrying Attacks to the Head

Shield Parry Position 1

Imagine an attack to your head, raise the shield so that the front face catches the sword, and the force of the strike slides the sword to the boss. Sometimes the force may turn the shield and then the opponent's sword is deflected to your right.

Make sure you can still see the opponent; do not blind yourself with the shield!

The optimum height of the shield is when the boss is level with the eyes, though change this according to your own body size.

The aim is to catch the blow on the flat of the shield.

Parrying Attacks to the Left Shoulder

Shield Parry Position 2

When an opponent attacks your left shoulder you need to raise and angle the shield so that flange (the flat part of the boss that sits against the wood) of the boss will catch the sword.

Make sure you can still see the opponent, do not blind yourself with the shield!

Raise the height of the shield so the boss is level with the left shoulder, this can change according to your own body size.

Aim to catch the sword on the metal rim of the boss.

Parrying Attacks to
the Right Shoulder

Shield Parry Position 3

Imagine the strike coming in from your right, extend the shield arm along the 45 degree angle that the shield is positioned in out to shoulder width.

Make sure you can still see the opponent, do not blind yourself with the shield!

You would catch the sword on your shield rim in the top right quarter. If the sword was sharp it would stick in the shield.

Parrying Attacks to the Left Thigh

Shield Parry Position 4

The strike will come from under toward your left thigh, with your shield on the left it is an easy parry.

Make sure you extend the arm, do not leave the shield touching the leg.

Extend the arm and drop the shield slightly, the sword strike should contact the flat of the shield between the boss and the rim.

Parrying Attacks to the Right Thigh

Shield Parry Position 5

The strike will come from below toward your right thigh, you must move the shield over a little to the right hand side, slightly lowering it.

Make sure you extend the arm, do not leave the shield touching the leg.

Push the shield out toward the right so that the rim is level with your right shoulder and slightly lower it. You would have caught the blow on the lower right quarter on the rim of your shield.

SECTION IV – SINGLE PERSON DRILLS

PRACTISING STRIKES AGAINST A TARGET WITH A HALF STEP

Drills 1 to 5

These simple drills are aimed to improve control of the sword and accuracy in striking a target. This is essential if you wish to fight against others.

Each drill practises a particular strike combined with a **Half Step** forward. **The sword strikes the target as the back foot ends the step.** You can also time this attack to hit when the front foot lands, it is up to you!

The sword moves from the start of your motion, so that your blade leads the attack.

This is very useful for a quick attack if someone steps too close in the fight.

Either leg can be forward, though without a shield it is safer to have the same leg forward as the sword hand.

Step and hit! As simple as that! If they somehow come closer still, you do not even need a step!

Calibration

We have already calibrated our distance to the target and marked them using lines taped on the floor as seen in the picture.

When you practise you must first calibrate the correct distance to the target. This is done by placing the

sword on the target with the side of the body forward which will be forward when you finish the actual swing of the sword. Then step back using the type of step you will use in the drill. In this case a half step with the left leg forward to start this drill.

This complete set of drills can be repeated with the right leg forward.

The picture to the left shows the position after this process has taken place.

Drill 1

Guard Position 1
Striking the Opponent's Head

Assume the normal guard position to attack the head, sword near the side of the head, with the point upward and angled slightly out of the vertical.

Using a half step with the front foot, step forward while starting your sword swing.

Strike straight and true! End your swing in the NRP 20 cm/ 8 inch from the target. Repeat as often as you need, become that Viking swordsman, strong, powerful and accurate!

SECTION IV. 1.

Drill 2

Guard Position 2
Striking the Opponent's
Left Shoulder
From the Guard position with the sword over the right shoulder, strike diagonally to the left shoulder of the imaginary opponent.

Half step forward with the front foot, while starting the sword swing, this gives you precise control of distance, repeat and hone that skill.

Remember, end the swing with the sword touching the target in the NRP, controlling the sword precisely! If you had not controlled your swing you could have cut him from the left shoulder through to the hip, like the warriors of old!

Drill 3

Guard Position 3
Striking the Opponent's
Right Shoulder

The sword is over the left shoulder ready to deliver a devastating blow to the un-shielded right shoulder of the opponent! Stand well balanced and ready.

Half stepping is natural with the front foot, and give you the timing to start your sword swing. Remember, distance judgement is vital for combat!

Hit the target with a controlled blow! Just touching while stopping the sword gives a safe environment for fighting. Repeat until that control is there, control the sword - control the fight!

Drill 4

Guard Position 4
Striking the Opponent's
Left Thigh

The sword is low under your right shoulder; you want to strike the opponent's left thigh a sneaky blow under the shield. Imagine the cut, make it happen!

Use the half step with the front foot, it is excellent for close in work, to control distance and timing!

This blow will catch them on the left thigh, it is hard to see it coming under the shield! Use the NRP to get the precision you need, safe and accurate, subtle and quick.

Drill 5

**Guard Position 5
Striking the Opponent's
Right Thigh**
This guard position is not used as often as the others. Sword behind your shield low on the left, ready to cut the opponent's right thigh. Remember your right side is exposed, be quick!

The opponent is close, cross the distance quickly with a half step with the front foot.

Swing the sword, contact as the step finishes. Timing is important to insure power and control!

SECTION IV. 1.

61

PRACTISING STRIKES AGAINST A TARGET WITH A FULL STEP

Drills 6 to 10

These drills practise your 5 strikes combined this time with a **Full Step** forward.

You can now fight at greater distance, and take the fight to the opponent! Remember this takes longer than the half step, so you have to time the attack well, maybe as he is stepping or changing guard position and therefore otherwise occupied.

A right handed person is better starting with the left leg forward in these drills, though you can execute them with the right leg forward and step with the left if you like.

While stepping, your balance can be easily upset; do not step too wide on wet terrain.

Calibration

We have already calibrated our distance to the target and marked it using lines taped on the floor, as seen in the picture.

When you practise, you must first calibrate the correct distance to the target. This is done by placing the sword on the target with the side

of the body forward which will be forward when you finish the actual swing of the sword. Then step back using the type of step you will use in the drill. In this case we use a full step, ending with the left leg forward to start the drill.

The picture to the left shows the position at the start of this process. The practitioner should now step back a full step to arrive at the calibrated position.

Drills 6

Guard Position 1
Striking the Opponent's Head

With the sword by your head, you will strike a straight blow to cleave the opponent's helmet in two! Actually better to control it and not hit, your sword companion will think better of it!

Start your sword swing, as you start to step. Twist the hips and shoulder toward the centre.

You must stop your sword in the NRP 20 cm/ 8 inch from the target if the head is unprotected. Make sure you stop the sword dead, no wobble or kink in the wrist. It takes practise; the lighter the sword, the easier it is.

SECTION IV. 2.

Drill 7

Guard Position 2
Striking the Opponent's
Left Shoulder

This diagonal sword blow starts over the right shoulder and travels in straight line to the left shoulder of the imaginary opponent. It is probably the most powerful blow and most commonly used to start the fight!

Stepping forward means the whole weight of the body is behind the blow, end in balance if you want to control the power. End the swing when the step ends!

The NRP is your control mechanism; you cannot fight safely without it. The warriors in the past would have cut the man to the left hip from the right shoulder with this blow! With training you could do no less, if you did not use that fine tuned control.

Drill 8

Guard Position 3
Striking the Opponent's
Right Shoulder
From above the left shoulder, the path of the cut will be to the opponent's un-shielded right shoulder! Focus your mind on making a precise cut, relaxed and powerful.

The full step takes longer, see the moment to step, is your opponent distracted? Cut quickly and maintain your balance. Your right side is uncovered!

Control that strike! Make light contact on the target, it is still a kill according to the rules. If you wanted, you could have added the power, though lost a friend! Everyone will thank you for precision and accuracy, use the NRP and be safe!

SECTION IV. 2.

Drill 9

Guard Position 4
Striking the Opponent's
Left Thigh

With the sword down on your right side, the idea is to strike a blow from below under their shield and into your opponent's thigh. This is a common fight finisher, often combatants do not see it coming!

Start to execute the cut just before stepping in. Coming from wide distance has its advantages though choose the right moment, maybe when he is changing guard!

Make each contact accurate and precise, you do not need a hammer, remember your sword is sharp! Just a touch is enough to show you have mastered control of the sword.

Drill 10

Guard Position 5
Striking the Opponent's
Right Thigh
The sword is partly hidden behind the shield on the left hand side. In the fight, the swing arc is directly to the opponent's right thigh. This blow takes courage and fortitude!

Time the cut and step as before. Concentrate on the target, you want to hit!

With controlled contact, you want to stop in the NRP, avoid a hard strike and end the fight! Remember soon you will be swinging that sword against your friend, make sure you have the skill of those ancient warriors!

SECTION V – PARTNER DRILLS

PARRYING WITH THE SWORD

Drills 1 to 5
These five blocks are the mainstay of your defence with the sword, you just need to learn these five and you defend against all the opponent's attacks!

We have purposefully copied the starting guard position of the opponent in each of these drills.

Start in any Guard position you like in your practise. We recommend that you try these defences from any position, you will quickly see which positions are more difficult to use.

Start at a distance so that your partner can hit you after taking **one full** step in every case. Calibrate that distance at the start.

We step back a **full step** in these examples, you might want to use a **half step** instead, depending upon the situation in the fight. Being out of distance is essential to staying safe.

Always attempt to parry with the Strong of your blade!

Drill 1

Parry Position 1
Sword Parry Against Attacks to the Head
Both start in guard position 1. The attacker initiates the movement, the defender reacts to the attack. The aim is a safe smooth parry, it is easy, your sword will do the work!

As the attacker moves to strike, turn your sword above your head, make that first parry position. Stay relaxed and cover your head!

As your sword comes to parry step back a full step, if you miss that parry you will still not be hit! Learn to move as well as block, movement is always useful in any fight.

69

Drill 2

Parry Position 2
Sword Parry Against Attacks to the Left Shoulder
Both players are starting in guard position 2. The attacker cuts to the left shoulder, you need to cover your left side!

As the attack develops, bring your hand down and across the body, twist your hips and shoulders, start to shift your weight onto your back leg in preparation for a step.

Remember leave the point of your sword in the centre, and parry while stepping back. Keeping safe out of distance combined with the parry, you cannot go wrong!

Drill 3

Parry Position 3
Sword Parry Against Attacks to the Right Shoulder

Here we start in guard position 3. As the attacker will strike for your right shoulder you will defend your right side!

Simply start to move your arm, hips and shoulders, so your arm comes across the body to cover the right hand side, shift your weight again to the back leg in preparation for a step backward.

Only move the sword level with the outside of the shoulder! The point stays fixed in the centre and the blade blocks the line. Step backward to complete the parry. After a parry, you are in a position to counter attack, remember that!

This photograph shows the relative positions of the fighter after the parry and step back. This is to show that you should be out of distance and is only for reference.

Drill 4

Parry Position 4
Sword Parry Against Attacks to the Left Thigh
With the sword under the right shoulder you have to move fast to parry the attack to your left thigh, it is easy after a little practise.

Turn the hand over, put the point of the sword down toward the ground. Twist the hips and shoulders and start to transfer the weight onto the rear leg.

Push your sword into the parry a little. Step back as you do so, and you will be safe on two counts! Parry and step.

Drill 5

**Parry Position 5
Sword Parry Against Attacks to
the Right Thigh**

The final position is under the left shoulder, guard number 5. This parry flows from this position, just remember to have the back of your hand in view the whole time!

Swing the sword forward to cover your right side, start twisting the hips and shoulders.

Step back as you parry, catching your opponent's blade in the strong of your sword. Make sure you can see the back of your sword hand, press into your opponent's blade a little for a powerful parry.

This photograph shows the relative positions of the fighter after the parry and step back. This is to show that you should be out of distance and is only for reference.

PARRYING WITH THE SHIELD

Drills 6 to 10

The shield is large, which means you do not have to move it very far to defend against any attack! It is also heavy so you want to move it as little as possible to be quicker than the sword!

We show the defender without sword to keep things simple. These parries are easy, you just have to keep your wits about you!

The defender can start in any guard position, it really makes little difference to him!

Remember if you miss the shield parry, you always step back a little out of range just to make sure. You can choose which step you should make, it is your fighting style after all.

The attacker will start in the appropriate guard position for each attack.

Drill 6

Parry Position 1
Parrying an Attack to the Head
The attacker starts and initiates the movement, the defender starts in any guard with the shield covering the left side of the body!

You have to cover your head without blinding yourself.

As the attacker moves to strike, start transferring your weight onto your rear leg. Raise that shield a little and start extending the arm.

Catch the blow between your front edge and your boss, extending your arm out, give yourself some space. Step back, if you miss that parry and you will still not be hit! You would now be ready to counter-attack in a fight.

Drill 7

Parry Position 2
Parrying an Attack to the
Left Shoulder
The attacker is wanting to attack your left shoulder. Your shield is almost there already!

The strike will come diagonally down on your left shoulder, you start by lifting and extending your arm. Don't forget to initiate the transfer the weight onto the back leg.

Finish by catching the sword near your boss with your arm extended and having stepped back. You are completely safe and you have set yourself up for a counter attack.

This photograph shows the relative positions of the fighter after the parry and step back. This is to show that you should be out of distance and is only for reference.

Drill 8

Parry Position 3
Parrying an Attack to the
Right Shoulder
The attacker wants to hit you on your right shoulder, you will parry with a small movement of the shield, blocking the line of the attack.

Your aim is to extend the front edge of the shield to cover the attacking line to the right shoulder. Start to shift weight to the rear leg.

Just push your arm out diagonally to the right about 20 cm/ 8 inch and catch the sword blow on the edge of your shield. This really shows how easy shield parrying is!

This photograph shows the relative positions of the fighter after the parry and step back. This is to show that you should be out of distance and is only for reference.

Drill 9

Parry Position 4
Parrying an Attack to the
Left Thigh
From guard position 4 the attacker wants to strike you on your left thigh. It is easy to parry though you must see it coming. Always hold your shield nearer your body when not about to parry.

Start by transferring the weight onto the rear leg, while extending your arm and dropping it slightly. If you do not step back remember you have to lower the shield even more!

After extending the arm, catch the
sword between the rim and the
boss, while retreating.

Drill 10

Parry Position 5
Parrying an Attack to the
Right Thigh
The fifth attack is to the right thigh, again this is not difficult to block, just do not extend the shield arm too far, opening up your left shoulder!

You are going to do as always, extend the shield arm and transfer weight. It is that simple.

There is hardly any need to drop the shield more than a few cm/inches and the line is covered. You have made your parry and stepped back for extra safety.

The photograph below shows the relative positions of the fighter after the parry and step back. This is to show that you should be out of distance and is only for reference.

Now you have learnt the parries with the shield, and you will agree they are really simple and easy to learn.

In the next section we combine parrying with the sword with parrying with the shield, we call it Zone defence. This really useful if assailed by more than one opponent at a time.

ZONAL DEFENSE WITH SWORD AND SHIELD

Drills 11 to 15

This type of defence is very useful when fighting two or more opponent's, or when you want to rest with the shield. You can also confuse an unwary attacker who thinks you will parry with the shield, though your parry with the sword. Later books will show you how to exploit this tactic!

As usual we will step backward with the parry, you can use a Full Step or a Half Step depending upon your opponent's fighting style.

Drill 11

Parry Position 1
Sword Parry against the Head Attack
Your attacker is going to strike you on the head! Use the sword here to parry so you can keep him in full view, and it is an ideal place from which to counter-attack.

Remember that the sword point lies slightly outside the width of your body.

Bring the sword point forward and raise the hand to get into position, ready your step backward by shifting the weight onto the rear leg.

The parry is done and you are safe. Think of ways to attack from here, with a step forward.

This photograph shows the relative positions of the fighter after the parry and step back. This is to show that you should be out of distance and is only for reference.

Drill 12

Parry Position 2
Shield Parry against the
Left Shoulder Attack
The natural defence to the expected
attack to your left shoulder is to use
your shield, as it is in the vicinity already.

As usual you need to extend the
shield arm, and prepare for the step
back.

Catch the blow on the shield face near the boss, your movement has secured your position from further immediate threat. Now you can play your game.

Drill 13

Parry Position 3
Sword Parry against the Right Shoulder Attack
You could block this attack to your right shoulder with the shield, it is easy. Though here we want to parry with the sword.

Bring the sword over to cover the right side and shift your weight ready to step.

Naturally, the parry is the same as before; you only have to remember to keep the point in your centre line. Do not forget to step back, use a full or half step, depending upon the situation.

Drill 14

Parry Position 4
Shield Parry against the Attack to the Left Thigh

It is most sensible to parry this attack with the shield as it is already nearly in place. Just watch out that he does not slip under your shield if you move too late!

The procedure is the same as all shield parries, start extending the arm and shifting your weight, by now it is too simple for words!

The shield will catch the sword blow underneath the boss, so it will not bounce up over your shield. Your step backward has secured your safety.

This photograph shows the relative positions of the fighter after the parry and step back. This is to show that you should be out of distance and is only for reference.

Drill 15

Parry Position 5
Sword Parry against the Attack to the Right Thigh

Here the attack switches back to the right side, and we switch the defence again to the sword.

In each of these Zonal defense drills your shield might be occupied defending against another attacker. The sword might be all you have to save yourself.

The sword should go to the right hand side while you step backward. You should see the back of your sword hand. Maintain your balance!

This parry has the sword point down toward the ground. It covers the attacking line to the whole leg. Get behind the sword and step out of range for added safety. Push into the parry slightly.

COMMON ERRORS
TO AVOID

Common Error 1

Incorrect sword parry against attack number 2
Firstly, the sword point is not on the centre line.

Secondly, the hips are not turned to the left enough, leading to the head twisting up slightly -- a very uncomfortable position!

Common Error 2

Incorrect sword parry against attack number 3
The sword point is not on the centre line. The sword arm is locked straight out, which is not good for the elbow and the parry will not absorb the energy of the blow easily.

The body is not straight, leaning backward also tends to throw the balance out.

Common Error 3

Incorrect position in a sword parry against attack number 4
The sword is pointing backward, so that is not defending the legs, it should be forward and vertical, pointing down to the floor.

The twist of the hips should be greater and the right arm aligned with the line of the oncoming blow.

This parry is easier if you step back with the left leg.

Common Error 4

Incorrect sword parry against attack number 5
The parry is too wide, and the sword is too far from the body. The sword arm is again locked straight. This is a false security.

The body is leaning too far forward.

Common Error 5

Incorrect shield parry against attack number 1
By raising the shield so the boss is on the centre line, the defender has blinded himself with the shield, he cannot see his opponent.

Theoretically this means he can never drop his shield again because he has no idea where the opponent's weapon is. A recipe for disaster!

Common Error 6

Incorrect shield parry against attack number 1 or number 2
The movement of the shield is too great, uncovering the intended defended areas, which in this case was the head. This also makes your arm tired quickly.

Exaggerated movement of the shield is one of the most common errors with both inexperienced and experienced fighters.

SECTION V. 4.

The student should learn to correct this as soon as possible.

Common Error 7

Incorrect shield parry against attack number 3
Using the face of the shield to parry has uncovered the rest of the body. The student should be using the edge in this position.

Also the movement of the shield is far too great.

Common Error 8

Incorrect shield parry against attack number 4
Here the fighter is trying to use the edge to parry, were he should be using the face.

He has uncovered the whole of his body to attack.

The body is leaning toward the shield, he should be standing straight.

Common Error 9

Incorrect shield defence against attack number 5
Here the fighter is trying to use the face of the shield to parry, were he should be using the edge.

The face of the shield is turned down so that the sword could slide off into his legs.

He has also uncovered the whole of his upper body to attack.

The body is leaning towards the shield, he should be standing straight.

SECTION V. 4.

AN EXAMPLE OF AN EXCHANGE OF BLOWS

Here we show a few attacks and defences in sequence, which should give the flavour of a fight. The blows are swapped as mentioned in the Viking Sagas, each fighter looking for the advantage over the other.

From the pictures it can be seen that it is advantageous to always parry an attack in a Guard position so you are immediately ready for a counter attack.

In your first fight just remember the simple things and do them well.

Always attempt to step back away from the attack if you have space.

Use small movements of the shield.

Extend the arm for parries with the shield or sword, though do not lock it out.

Remember your stance and balance, if it is good everything will look and feel good. That is an excellent place to be.

Guard Positions
The fighter in Brown starts with the sword over the head in Position 1.

The fighter in Red chooses to start with the sword under the right shoulder in Position 4.

Choice of guard position is a personal thing based on experience and tactical choices. We will touch on this subject more in each book.

Brown

Red

First Strike

Brown takes the initiative and strikes the first cleaving blow toward the slightly exposed left shoulder of Red. Red steps back with a half step and raises the face of his shield to defend against the attack.

You can see that Red has made a slight mistake, because he only took a half step backward Browns sword is still in reach! It is a good job his shield work was fast enough to catch the blow.

Red Returns the Favour

Having survived Brown's attack the initiative passes to Red, because Brown must ready his sword in a position to strike again, usually from a guard position.

Red defended in guard Position 2, so is immediately ready to strike after Browns blow is stopped.

This is one of the great advantages of having a two weapon system such as Sword and Shield.

have been better to make a full step, but this would have taken longer and allowed Brown more time to react.

These decisions are always a matter of experience and also depend upon a fighter's assessment of his opponent.

Brown immediately makes a full step backward and pushes his shield out diagonally to the right, intercepting the attack with the top right quarter of his shield. This is a perfect ex-

Remember the person who has the initiative and moves first to attack will cause problems to the defender. The defender always needs a certain reaction time before he can start his own moves!

Red chooses to strike at the undefended right shoulder of Brown, while stepping forward again with a half step to the left. This step to the left gives more chance to reach the right shoulder of Brown. It might

ample of this type of shield parry. Brown is a tall man and his large step takes him out of danger. Red will have to take larger steps to keep up with him!

Brown Counters to the Head

Brown quickly recovers, and from Position 2, cuts to Red's head.

He has no intention of contacting the head as this is not allowed when there is no hard protection, though this attack must be practiced because you never know what may happen, especially when fighting strangers or people with very little control.

Red goes back a full step while raising his shield into shield defence 1

Red goes for the Opening.

Because Red did not blind himself with the shield, he sees that Brown has an open right side, not actually defended by anything.

Stepping with the back leg forward and slightly to the left, he cuts again to the right shoulder of Brown.

He chooses this target as it will force Brown to move his shield a large distance, he hopes that his opponent will over-parry and therefore be

edge and does not over-parry, he also drops his sword down to cover a possible attack under his shield.

to block the downward blow. Breathing in, he pulls his sword back to be ready for his next blow.

Brown is in a very forward position and has exposed his whole right side.

out of position to deal with his second blow.

If Brown makes a mistake and parries with the face of his shield he will finish in a tactically bad position. Fortunately Brown uses his shield

Red Throws a Second Blow

Red has a momentary advantage because Brown is not in a proper guard position and his sword is not ready to use.

Red makes a large diagonal full step to the right and tries to strike under Browns shield into the left thigh.

Brown is quick to see the move of Red, and steps back a full step while lowering his shield. This step backward gives him the time to ex-

Here we leave this engagement as it seems these two opponent's are equally matched. It may be a long time before we see a result.

ecute the parry. Note here he correctly uses the face of the shield to block the blow.

CONCLVSIONS

We hope that you have seen that this system is simple to learn and to put into practise! That is the key word here Practise! Practise! Practise!

Train on the pell, train with a friend, the more you do the better you get! Simple as that!

The prime concern is safety, we achieve that through using the NRP to stop the sword exactly in the same place every time and by always stepping away from an attack.

Once you are safe you can expand your skills and your horizons. The next step, Beginners Guide 2, will be plain sailing.

Don't forget to check out the companion DVD to go with this book.

We are also looking into starting an online school where you can download videos and train. Constantly improving your skills through feedback and repetition.

Colin Richards also gives seminars on various weapon combinations used in the Viking era. Viking spear and shield fighting, two handed spear combat, two weapon systems including sword with sword, sword with axe, and axe with axe. Not to forget the fearsome two handed axe sometimes called the Dane Axe.

Look at our web sight for any special offers, such as free book and DVD seminars.

These seminar are relevant for experienced and inexperienced fighters. If you have enough people, you can organise a seminar and Colin will travel to your location and instruct.

See our web site
www.ArtsofMars.com
for more information
or email
info@ArtsofMars.com

We look forward to seeing you at a seminar in the future.

Enjoy your fighting and stay safe. We welcome feed back and questions, so please drop us a line.

Arts of Mars Books
Colin Richards
Publishing House
Badestraße 14
31020 Salzhemmendorf
Germany
www.ArtsOfMarsBooks.com
Email: books@artsofmars.com
phone: 0049-5153- 803253

Arts of Mars Books is a new publishing house specializing in producing books and videos on the subject of European Historical Martial Arts. Interest in this field is growing as more and more old treatises on weapon use are found in the world's libraries.

We are dedicated to producing high quality products of innovative design. Though you can only really learn a martial art from an instructor we think that with correctly designed books and DVD's can augment that learning and also give a good basic grounding for further development.

Our Beginners Guide books and DVD's are designed to give a good grounding for students to develop their technical expertise from. We hope we have achieved our goal.

Book
Fiore dei Liberi 1409
Wrestling & Dagger

This book covers the Wrestling and Dagger techniques of Fiore dei Liberi from the "Getty" version of the "Fior di Battaglia". Included is a selection of the 'Pisani-Dossi' "Flos Duellatorum" dagger techniques.

All techniques are described in both English and German. Using a unique Timeline system, the photographs in the book detail the stages of each technique as they occur in time, with a separate close up focus on hand and foot movements, each positioned in the Timeline at the correct place. Included are floor grid lines so that foot movements can be easily followed at every stage. No more wondering where the feet have moved!

Product details
Hardcover: 921 pages, full colour
Product Dimensions: 30 x 21,3 x 1,8 cm
Author: Colin Richards
Language English & German
Release Date May 2007
ISBN 978-3-9811627-0-7
Price 44,95 Euro

DVD
Medieval Combat,
Italian Longsword
Student Guide- Level 1

The Medieval Knight was a carefully trained fighting machine, armed primarily with a superbly designed lightweight hand and a half sword. The Italian Martial Arts Master Fiore dei Liberi wrote his highly effective fighting techniqes down for future generations to delve into the mysteries of the world of knighly combat.

We present this valuable cultural heritage in three DVDs, the first of which "Student Guide - Level 1" includes the following: Gripping the Sword, Breathing Technique, Stance Turning, Tactical Stepping, Basic Guard Positions, Cutting with the Sword, Thrusting with the Sword, Distance, Single Person Drills, Partner Drills and Exercises.

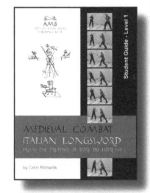

Product details
Language: English Sound: Dolby
NTSC 4:3 Digital
Producer: Colin und Sandra Richards
Release Date August 2009
Run Time: 1 hour 50 min
ISBN 978-3-9811627-1-4
Price 39,90 Euro

More Products coming in 2011

Book:
Performing Better by Improving Your Training Methods
Applying Sport Sciences to Martial Arts and Combat Sports
By Luis Preto

Book:
Medieval Sword and Buckler Fighting
Beginners Guide Level 1
By Colin Richards

DVD:
Companion Volume to the book:
Viking Sword and Shield Fighting
Beginners Guide Level 1
By Colin Richards

AMB
Arts of Mars Books
Colin Richards
www.ArtsOfMarsBooks.com

Seelenschmiede, Stefan Roth
Klostergang 56
38104 Braunschweig
Germany
www.seelenschmiede.de
Email: info@seelenschmiede.de
phone: 0049-171- 5404455

Stefan Roth is a master sword maker of very high standard. These photographs are a testament to his skill and dedication. He believes in perfect swords and strives to reach this goal with every sword he makes. Each is unique.

Gothic Long Sword

Cavalry Sword

Ring Pommel Sword

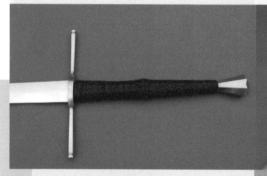
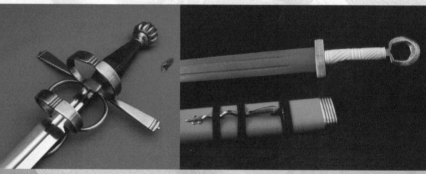

His swords are works of art and are finished with the utmost care. They are polished to perfection and sharpened to what ever edge bevel you wish. Test cutting with these swords is a pleasure you do not want to miss.

We have never handled a Stefan Roth sword we did not want to own. Go to his web site and see for yourself, truly wonderful to behold.